Alan Titchmarsh's

PRUNING

HAMLYN

London · New York · Sydney · Toronto

Cutting Remarks

There are no two ways about it: pruning is one of the most terrifying jobs in the garden. A sharp pair of secateurs in one hand and a stem in the other are guaranteed to strike terror into the hardest heart. One snip and it's gone, never to be stuck back on again!

The greatest difficulty is deciding just *how* to prune a shrub or fruit tree or whether to prune it at all. After all, Nature never prunes her plants, and they grow well enough, don't they? Or do they? Take a closer look at wild trees and shrubs. Often as not they'll have a few dead stems that are beginning to let in disease. They might not be very shapely either. In short, they're a delight at a distance but they wouldn't stand up to close scrutiny in the garden. Pruning is definitely necessary, but each plant's individual requirements must be met.

It's easy to say 'if in doubt, cut it out', but this is a maxim that can have disastrous effects. Some shrubs do need to be regularly hacked back to give of their best, but others prefer to be left alone. This little book offers an at-a-glance guide to the pruning needs of a wide range of garden plants. Check what each one needs, and hopefully you'll never have to make the unkindest cut of all.

Why prune – and when?

There are several reasons why pruning is necessary:
- To keep the plant healthy
- To keep the plant shapely and within bounds
- To encourage flowering and fruiting
- To encourage stem and leaf growth

Health

Every now and then plant stems die, maybe as a result of damage, attack by a pest or disease, or because the plant is, for some reason, unable to support them. If you leave dead stems on the plant, not only will they look unsightly but they will probably result in further damage when fungus diseases colonise the rotting tissue. They should always be cut out well back into healthy growth.

Left with a dense canopy of overcrowded stems, some shrubs will be prone to fungus diseases which will enjoy the stagnant conditions in the centre of the bush where air has a job to circulate. Thinning out the stems will improve plant health. This is especially true with roses which are susceptible to mildew and blackspot.

Obviously, any stem you see that is already diseased should quickly be snipped out before the infection spreads. A few quick cuts may save the life of your plant.

Shape and size

Generally speaking, the harder you cut a plant back, the more vigorously it will grow. This is a state of affairs which the pruner can use to advantage. Plants that are required to produce new stems each year (either for foliage or flowers) will respond to hard pruning: buddleias, roses, ornamental-leafed dogwoods and the like. Plants that bloom on older growth will be ruined by hard pruning and their natural shape destroyed: magnolias, witch hazels and rhododendrons. But with almost any shrub, an occasional branch can be removed if it gets in the way or restricts access to a path, or generally makes the bush lop-sided. The secret is to cut it out completely, right back to its point of origin.

Buddleia is pruned hard back in winter or early spring

Never hack back all the stems on a shrub uniformly, unless you are certain that such pruning will produce a better, more floriferous plant. It is almost always best to thin out the stems, removing a few old and gnarled ones completely, so that the overall shape and grace of the plant is retained.

Flowering and fruiting

You'll have to know which kind of wood your shrub blooms on before you take the secateurs to it. Does it bloom on shoots made in the previous year? Does it bloom on shoots made during the current year? Or does it flower on little sideshoots or 'spurs' that occur on older stems? Fruits follow flowers, so the pruning is responsible for the production of both.

As a general rule:

● Shrubs that flower on the current season's growth are pruned in winter, cutting the stems really hard back, e.g. bush roses, buddleia.

● Shrubs that flower on one-year old wood are pruned immediately after flowering, when the flowered stems are cut out completely and the new growths allowed to replace them, e.g. philadelphus, forsythia.

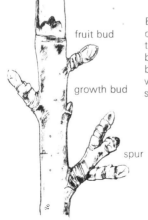

fruit bud

growth bud

spur

Build up a spur system on cordon apples to encourage the production of fat fruit buds. The smaller growth buds give rise to new shoots which are shortened back in summer to form new spurs

- Shrubs that flower on spurs produced on older wood can have their sideshoots shortened in summer to encourage spur production, e.g. cordon apples, chaenomeles.
- Shrubs that flower regularly on stems that are over one year old need only be pruned to remove dead, diseased, overcrowded or badly shaped stems, e.g. magnolia, hamamelis.

Stems and leaves

Except on those shrubs which flower on the current season's wood, hard pruning will encourage the production of stem and leaf growth. Gardeners who panic and hack back their philadelphus every winter will know this to be true – it will produce a thicket of leafy stems but no flowers, for the stems are never allowed to reach an age of one year and come into bloom.

Snipping back to encourage leaf production is an advantage with some plants, such as variegated dogwoods and willows grown for their colourful stems. Here the young foliage and stems are the plants' principal attractions and they can be positively enhanced by pruning.

Always remember to cut out plain green 'reverted' stems on variegated plants, and prune evergreens in spring rather than winter so that they can then burst straight into growth rather than sitting and sulking.

There's one rule worth remembering about shoot growth, and that is this: the shoot tip produces chemicals which are passed back down the stem to inhibit the growth of the lower buds. Nip out the shoot tip and the production of the chemical is stopped, allowing the lower buds to grow. The removal of a shoot tip will always encourage bushiness.

Tree pruning

Apart from a simple bit of dead-wooding, tree pruning is really a job for a qualified tree surgeon. Such a specialist is hardly likely to knock on your door asking for work; you will have to seek him out in your local telephone directory. *Never* agree to let an odd-job man prune your trees. He'll like as not leave you heart broken and your trees in a mess.

Select the right tree at the outset and only in its early years should it need pruning. Snip off small twigs and branches that appear up the first 2 m (6 ft) of stem, to leave a clean trunk and bole. Spread the job over two or three years if your like.

It's also vitally important to make sure that any young tree has a 'leader' – a strong central shoot that will eventually become the main trunk. If your tree loses its leader, make sure that another one is encouraged to take over from it. Prune out any competitors.

Timing

The timing of pruning depends on the points already mentioned: the kind of wood to be encouraged or retained. As a rule, pruning is carried out in winter, early spring or immediately after flowering. Some plants, though, respond to summer pruning (apples trained as cordons, for instance), and with one or two trees, summer pruning reduces the bleeding that can occur when the sap rises in spring. The A to Z section on page 10 gives more details.

Tools and techniques

You'll need three basic pieces of equipment:

● Secateurs
● Loppers
● Pruning saw

The secateurs can be of the anvil or scissor type, but whatever they are they should be sharp and clean and well oiled.

Loppers are those long-handled secateurs which are used to cut stems thicker than your finger.

A pruning saw usually has a curved blade and cuts on the 'pull' stroke. The narrow blade can get into crowded shrubs much more easily than a conventional saw.

Hedge owners will need sharp and comfortable shears.

Cutting

● Never cut a stem thicker than the secateurs or loppers can manage. Use the right tool for the right job.
● Always make pruning cuts just above an outward-facing bud, sloping back slightly from it.
● Never leave budless snags; they will only die back.
● When thinning a shrub, remove unwanted stems completely, either back to their point of origin on an older stem, or right back to the ground. Stubs that are left will rot, look unsightly, and cut your hands next time you prune.
● When cutting a large branch from a tree, reduce its weight by cutting off the end before you make the final cut against the trunk or older branch.
● Paint all cut surfaces larger than 2.5 cm (1 in) diameter with a proprietary wound sealant.

Forsythia is pruned immediately after flowering

A to Z of garden trees and shrubs

Abutilon Cut faded flowerheads from *A. vitifolium*. Cut out completely a few old stems from *A. megapotamicum* each spring.

Acacia Cut out dead or damaged stems in spring.

Acer (Japanese maple) Snip off dead stem ends in spring. Other pruning is seldom necessary, but branches which have to be removed should be cut off in late summer to avoid bleeding.

Arbutus (Strawberry tree) Remove dead shoots in spring. When growths are killed, prune the stems hard back in spring to shoots that can be seen bursting from the older wood.

Artemisia Cut back all artemisias to shoots that are growing from just above ground level in spring.

Aucuba (Spotted laurel) Cut out completely any dead growths in spring. Remove unwanted shoots at the same time, though unless grown as a hedge, regular pruning is not necessary.

Bamboos Prune only if you're fastidious, removing a few dead canes each spring but leaving some of them to support the new growths. Bamboos do *not* die completely after flowering.

Berberis (Barberry) Pruning is not essential but dead shoots can be cut out in summer. Overgrown bushes can be chopped off at ground level in spring to re-grow. Clip hedges of *B. × stenophylla* after flowering.

Betula (Birch) Make sure that only one 'leader' is allowed to grow; snip out shoots that compete in summer. Remove any shoots that sprout from the trunk to leave 2 or 2.5 m (6 or 7 ft) of clear stem. These, too, should be cut off in summer and the job can be spread over two years.

Buddleia (Butterfly bush)   Cut back *B. davidii* to within a few inches of ground level in early spring. Remove some older stems from *B. globosa* each year in late winter, leaving the shoot tips intact on other stems. After flowering cut back the stems of *B. alternifolia* to new shoots which are beginning to grow.

Buxus (Box)   Clip hedges and trained specimens in summer. Old and overgrown plants will sometimes produce new growth if cut back almost to ground level in late spring.

Calluna (Heather)   Clip over the plants in spring, removing about half the previous year's growth. Cut to just above young shoots, not into old wood.

Camellia   No regular pruning necessary. Cut out dead or damaged growth in spring. Old and leggy plants can be cut back hard to sprouting buds at the same time.

Carpinus (Hornbeam)   Clip hedges in summer.

Caryopteris (Blue spiraea)   Cut back hard to buds breaking just above ground level in spring.

Ceanothus (Californian lilac)   With evergreen species, shorten the sideshoots by one third after flowering and remove one or two old stems in spring if the bush needs thinning out. Deciduous kinds are left unpruned for the first two years to build up a framework. Each succeeding spring the previous season's growth is cut back to two buds as soon as these can be seen bursting into growth.

Chaenomeles (Cydonia; japonica; Japanese quince) With wall-trained plants, cut back to 15 cm (6 in) any shoots that grow straight out from the plants in summer. Further shorten these shoots to two buds in winter. The plant flowers on spurs produced on old wood, but one or two old and overcrowded stems can be removed in spring if required. Free-standing specimens need no regular pruning.

Chamaecyparis (False cypress)   No pruning is needed with free-standing plants that have room to grow. When used as a hedging plant, cut out the top once the plant has passed its desired height. Clip lightly once a year in late spring or early summer.

Chimonanthus (Winter sweet)   Too much pruning results in too little flower. Remove an old stem in spring occasionally. When wall trained, shoots which grow straight out can be shortened to two buds in late winter.

Choisya (Mexican orange blossom)   Cut back flowered shoots by 30 cm (1 ft) to encourage a later flush of bloom. Cut back hard any winter-damaged stems in spring.

Cistus (Sun rose)   Snip off dead growths in spring. No other pruning should be needed.

Clematis (Virgin's bower)   There are three systems of pruning which relate to the following habit of the plants:
1. The early-flowerers need pruning only if they are taking up too much space. Snip out all shoots that have flowered as soon as the blooms fade: e.g. *C. alpina*, *C. montana*, *C. macropetala*.
2. In this group belong the large-flowered varieties that start to bloom before the middle of June. Prune in late winter cutting back all shoots to fat and healthy buds. Cut out any dead growth. e.g. Nelly Moser, Mrs Cholmondeley, Barbara Dibley, Barbara Jackman, Lasurstern, The President.
3. The later, large-flowering varieties are also pruned in late winter. Cut back the stems to within 60 or 100 cm (2 or

Sweetly-scented chimonanthus needs little pruning

3 ft) of the ground, just above a healthy pair of buds. e.g. Jackmanii, Ville de Lyon, Perle d'Azur, Ernest Markham.

Cornus (Dogwood)   Those that are grown for colourful stems and leaves should be cut back to just above soil level in late winter. Larger types grown for flowers need be relieved only of dead wood in spring.

Corylus (Hazel)   Weak shoots can be snipped out in winter and if new growth is required, old stems can be cut out at ground level at the same time. Hazel suckers freely.

Cotinus (Smoke bush)   Bushes can be left unpruned but will make better foliage plants if allowed to grow to 60 cm (2 ft) and then cut hard back to leave just two or three buds of new growth in spring. This system is especially useful on purple-leaved forms.

Cotoneaster   Regular pruning is seldom needed. Cut out completely any unwanted or encroaching stems in spring to maintain the graceful habit. Cut cotoneaster hedges with secateurs in spring.

Crataegus (Hawthorn; quick)   Trees need little or no pruning, other than to remove branches which make access a hazard. Clip hedges in summer.

× **Cupressocyparis** (Leyland cypress)   As for *Chamaecyparis*.

Cupressus (Cypress)   As for *Chamaecyparis*.

Cytisus (Broom)   The popular varieties of broom can be pruned after flowering – cut out the flowered stems so that about half the previous season's growth is removed, along with the developing pods. Never cut back into thick, old stems. *C. battandieri* (Moroccan broom) can be relieved of one or two old stems each spring.

Daboecia (St Dabeoc's heath)   As for *Calluna*.

Deutzia   Cut out a few of the older stems at ground level immediately after flowering. In winter some of the thin and twiggy shoots that clog the centre of the bush can be removed.

Elaeagnus No regular pruning necessary, though stems which grow where they are not wanted can be cut out completely in spring. Remove green shoots from variegated varieties at the same time.

Erica (Heath) Varieties that flower in summer, autumn and winter should be pruned in spring as the new shoots start to grow. Spring-flowering varieties should be pruned as the flowers fade. With all of them, lightly clip over to remove the flowered stems just above newly breaking shoots.

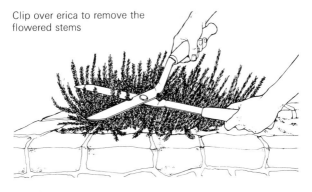

Clip over erica to remove the flowered stems

Eucalyptus (Gum tree) Cut back dead shoots to growing buds in spring. Young plants can be shortened to 45 cm (18 in) after planting to encourage a strong root system and good branch framework. Prune annually in this fashion if you want a shrubby plant.

Mop-headed hydrangeas are pruned in early spring

Euonymus Neither deciduous nor evergreen types need any regular pruning. Unwanted stems of deciduous kinds can be cut out completely in spring; encroaching stems of evergreens can be shortened at the same time.

Euphorbia (Spurge) Remove old, flowered stems in autumn, cutting them out at their bases.

Fagus (Beech) Clip hedges annually in summer.

Fatsia (False castor oil) Prune only to remove dead stems and leaves in spring. This plant is occasionally killed back to soil level in severe winters.

Forsythia Cut out completely several of the older stems immediately after flowering.

Fuchsia Cut back the stems by half in autumn to reduce wind rock. Cut all stems back to healthy, sprouting buds in spring (to ground level or higher as required).

Garrya Cut out stems that grow straight forward from wall-trained plants in late winter.

Genista Pruning of *G. cinerea* is as for cytisus. Other species seldom need pruning (and are spoilt by it) except to remove dead wood in spring.

Hamamelis (Witch hazel) Seldom, if ever, pruned.

Hebe (Shrubby veronica) Prune in spring when growth is scraggy or has been killed by frost. Cut back hard to just above buds which are beginning to sprout.

Hedera (Ivy) Clip wall-trained specimens with shears in spring or early summer when they become thick and heavy (see page 18).

Helianthemum (Rock rose) Snip back long or untidy growths after flowering.

Hibiscus Cut out dead wood in spring. Overgrown and elderly plants can be cut hard back in spring when the breaking buds can be seen.

Hydrangea Plants of *H. paniculata grandiflora* should be cut back to the lowest pair of buds on the previous season's growth in late winter. The mop-headed varieties of *H. macrophylla*, the commonest garden hydrangeas, are pruned in early spring. Cut out completely one or two very old and any very weak stems at ground level. Remove faded flowerheads, cutting back to just above a

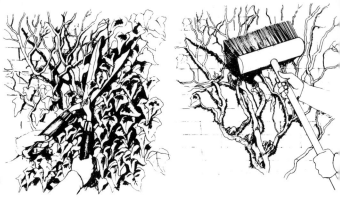

Clip ivy growing against a wall and then brush over to get rid of any dirt and loose material (see page 17)

strong pair of buds. The fat terminal buds produce the flowers. Leave on faded flowerheads as winter protection, except with lacecap varieties where they can be snipped off as they fade. Other species can be relieved of one or two old stems, and any weak growths, in spring. *H. petiolaris*, the climbing hydrangea, can be relieved of shoots which grow straight out from the wall in summer.

Hypericum (St John's wort; Rose of Sharon)   Cut back *H. calycinum* to ground level in early spring. Other species can be pruned free of spindly stems and have healthy shoots shortened a little to healthy buds at the same time.

Ilex (Holly)   Clip hedges in summer. Cut back unwanted branches on free-standing plants at the same time.

Jasminum (Winter jasmine)   Cut out completely any flowered shoots as soon as the blooms fade.

Juniperus (Juniper)   Remove dead growths.

Kerria (Jew's mallow)   Cut out a few of the older stems as soon as the flowers fade.

Kolkwitzia (Beauty bush)   Cut out a few old and weak stems immediately after flowering.

Laburnum   Unwanted branches should be removed in late summer. Seedheads can be snipped off as the flowers fade. Laburnums trained over arches and pergolas can be tied in and have their sideshoots shortened to two buds in early winter.

Laurus (Sweet bay)   Snip back the shoots of topiary bays in summer – several times if necessary. Cut out dead shoots in spring.

Lavandula (Lavender)   Remove flowerheads as they fade. Cut back each year in spring to buds that are breaking low down on the stems.

Lavatera (Tree mallow)   Cut hard back to within a few inches of ground level in spring, when new shoots can be seen growing there.

Ligustrum (Privet)   Clip hedges with shears once or twice in summer.

Lippia (Lemon-scented verbena)   Cut back to breaking buds in spring. The plant is killed back to soil level in most winters.

Lonicera (Honeysuckle)   Clip over hedges of *L. nitida* (an evergreen species) in summer. The common honeysuckle, *L. periclymenum*, is pruned by cutting out a few of the older, flowered stems just as the blooms fade (if you can get near enough). Do not remove the young stems which will carry flowers the following year. *L. japonica* and its varieties can be hard clipped in spring.

Magnolia   Remove only dead stems in spring. When pruning is necessary do the job in summer, removing some stems completely and shortening others to just above a leaf or bud.

Mahonia Long and leggy stems of mahonias such as 'Charity' can be shortened drastically in early spring to encourage a bushy habit.

Osmanthus Unwanted or overlong stems can be cut back in late spring. Large and ungainly stems of considerable age can be cut out after flowering.

Parthenocissus (Virginia creeper; Boston ivy) Cut out unwanted stems in autumn to reduce weight and spread.

Pernettya Cut out dead or dying stems in spring.

Philadelphus (Mock orange; syringa) Cut out a few old stems at ground level immediately after flowering.

Phlomis (Jerusalem sage) Overgrown plants can be cut hard back to breaking buds in spring.

Pieris (Flame of the forest) Only unwanted, damaged or encroaching stems need be cut out in spring.

Pittosporum Overgrown or snow-damaged plants can be cut hard back in spring, either to within a few inches of older growth or near to ground level.

Polygonum (Russian vine; mile-a-minute) Cut back unwanted stems in spring.

Potentilla Snip back thin and weak shoots to a couple of buds in spring. Shorten stronger stems by half.

Prunus (Flowering cherry; laurel) Clip laurel in summer. Overgrown plants can be cut hard back to stumps in spring. Flowering cherries need only be pruned to rid them of dead or diseased wood. *P. tenella*, the dwarf Russian almond, falls into the same category. *P. triloba* is often grown against a wall. Any shoots which grow outwards should be cut back to two buds after flowering.

Pyracantha (Firethorn) Cut out completely any

Osmanthus and chaenomeles trained against a wall

invasive branches in spring. Hedges or wall-trained plants can be close-clipped in spring but flower and berry production will be reduced.

Rhododendron (Including azalea) Remove dead flowers as soon as they fade. Dead wood can be cut out in summer. Hedges of *R. ponticum* can be close-pruned in summer.

Rhus (Stag's horn sumach) Cut out only dead wood in spring if a large specimen is wanted. It can be kept shrubby by cutting hard back to just above a breaking bud in spring.

Ribes (Flowering currant) Cut out several older branches after flowering. Hedges can be clipped after flowering.

Rosa (Rose) Prune according to type:

Hybrid teas   Prune in late winter or early spring. Cut out dead, diseased and a portion of older wood. Remove also any crossing branches so that the centre of the bush is open. Snip out spindly shoots. Reduce the half dozen or so stems that are left to just below knee height, cutting just above outward-facing buds. Newly planted hybrid teas should be shortened to within 8 or 10 cm (3 or 4 in) of ground level, again cutting to just above outward-facing buds.

Floribundas   The same as for hybrid teas, but reduce to just above knee height, rather than just below. With both types remove faded flowerheads to encourage further flushes of bloom. Cut back newly planted floribundas to within 15 cm (6 in) of soil level.

Standard roses   Prune as for hybrid tea and floribunda roses but for 'soil level', read 'the top of the main stem'.

Shrub roses   Generally little pruning is required, other than the removal of dead or diseased stems in winter. One or two overcrowded or spindly stems can be cut out completely at the same time.

Miniature roses   Thin out overcrowded stems and snip off dead shoot tips in early spring.

Ramblers   One or two old stems can be removed completely, if practical. Trim back sideshoots to three buds. Prune in autumn.

Climbers   Cut out dead and worn-out stems. Snip off dead shoot tips and shorten sideshoots to three buds. Prune in late winter.

Rosmarinus (Rosemary)   Cut back overgrown or damaged plants quite hard in spring.

Salix (Willow)   Species that are grown as bushes for colourful winter stems should be cut back to ground level in late winter or early spring. Dwarf willows need no regular pruning other than the removal of dead wood.

Salvia (Sage)   Cut back the stems quite hard in spring. New shoots will arise from stem bases.

Sambucus (Elder)   The coloured-leaved forms of the elder can be kept in good condition by removing completely a few older stems each year. The young ones that remain are shortened by half.

Santolina (Lavender cotton)   Cut hard back to shoots breaking at the base of the plant in spring. This makes a good dwarf hedge which can be clipped over twice in summer. Unless clipped off, the flowers will pull the bush open.

Senecio (Dusty miller)   The bushy S. 'Sunshine', often known as *S. greyi*, is best given a hard pruning back into old wood every three or four years. Dead flowerheads should be removed annually.

Spartium (Spanish broom)   Cut back the previous season's growth to within one or two buds of the older wood in spring. Aged bushes can be hard pruned almost

Pruning a hybrid tea rose; floribundas are cut back rather less drastically

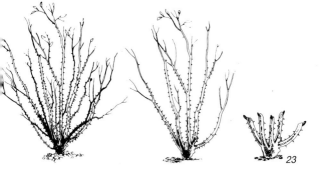

Cut coloured-stemmed willows down to the ground in spring

to ground level.

Spiraea For species such as *S.* × *arguta* and *S. thunbergii*, which flower on stems made during the previous year, cut out a few older stems each winter. Species which flower on stems made during the same season (such as *S.* × *bumalda* 'Anthony Waterer') should be cut back to a few inches in spring.

Syringa (Liliac; see also *Philadelphus*) Cut off faded flowerheads immediately they go over. Remove suckers that emerge from the base of the plant. Unwanted stems can be cut out in winter.

Tamarix (Tamarisk) Cut back the shoots of late summer-flowering species to within a few buds of older wood in spring. Shorten the long, flowered stems on spring-flowering species as the blooms fade.

Taxus (Yew) Clip in early summer. Old and decrepit yews can be cut hard back to stumps in spring. New growth will sprout from the old stems.

Viburnum Unwanted stems on deciduous and evergreen species can be cut out in spring, though no regular pruning is necessary on most of them. *V. tinus* can be clipped over in spring to encourage bushiness. *V. fragrans* can be relieved of a few older stems each spring.

Vitis (Ornamental vine) Cut out unwanted stems in early winter and shorten all sideshoots to three buds.

Weigela (Diervilla; bush honeysuckle) Cut out a few older stems immediately after flowering. Snip out weak and spindly shoots in winter.

Wisteria Shorten unwanted stems back to six leaves in summer. Shorten all sideshoots to three buds in winter, and cut back to the same degree any long stems that are not needed to extend the branch framework.

A to Z of fruit trees and bushes

Apples and pears   The type of pruning depends on the form of tree being grown. Most apples and pears fruit on small sideshoots known as 'spurs' and it is these that are encouraged by careful pruning. Some varieties fruit at the stem tips (Bramley's Seedling is one) and with these tip bearers half the sideshoots or laterals should be left unpruned.

Bush apples and pears   Newly planted two- or three-year-old bushes should have all their shoots shortened by one half in winter. Cut to just above an outward-facing bud. The following winter, cut back the previous summer's growth by half. From the next year onwards, only the sideshoots need be pruned. Cut them back to 10 cm (4 in) during the winter. Annual pruning is desirable but not essential. Standard and half-standard trees are pruned in the same way.

Cordon apples and pears   Here the trees are grown on a single stem tilted at an angle of 45 degrees. They are usually grown against 2-m (6-ft) high post-and-wire fences. Established cordons are pruned in summer. Cut back the sideshoots to three leaves so that a spur system is built up. Cut off the top of the main shoot when it reaches the top of the training wires.

Espalier apples and pears   These trees have horizontal tiers of branches. Summer prune the shoots as for cordons so that fruiting spurs are produced. When too many spurs are present they can be thinned out in winter.

The fruit on apples and pears can be thinned if the crop is very heavy. It's a fiddly job but it does help to avoid alternate years of heavy and light cropping. Snip off a few fruits from each cluster when the natural fruit drop has occurred in early summer.

Blackberries and loganberries   Cut out fruiting stems once the crop has been picked. Best grown on a post-and-wire fence. The fruiting stems or canes can be spaced out fan-wise and the new growth taken up the centre in a tall column. When the fruiting stems are cut out, lower the new ones and space them out to replace them.

Blackcurrants   Do not prune after the first year's growth. Subsequently any spindly stems plus a few old stems can be cut out each winter. This maintains a regular supply of healthy young wood which will start to fruit when one year old. All stems that are removed should be cut out cleanly at ground level.

Pruning a blackcurrant bush

Apple variety Lord Lambourne grown as an espalier

Red and white currants The ideal red or white currant has a goblet-shaped arrangement of six or eight branches. Pruning aims to encourage the production of fruiting sideshoots (quite a different state of affairs to that in blackcurrants). Remove one or two of the oldest stems each year in winter. Shorten all sideshoots to six leaves in summer.

Morello cherries Most cherries are too large for small gardens, but the acid, or morello, cherry can be fan-trained against a north-facing wall. Rig up a system of horizontal wires that can be held at intervals of 45 cm (18 in) up the face of the wall with screw eyes. Cherries are best pruned in spring or summer, rather than winter when silver leaf disease may strike. Thin out the shoot system in summer, removing shoots that are growing directly away from the wall, any that are weak and spindly or generally overcrowded. Space the remainder 15 cm (6 in) apart and tie them in. Once the crop has been picked, cut back the fruiting sideshoots and allow the young shoots that have grown from their bases to replace them. When young growths are rare, one or two older stems can be cut back to suitable laterals to encourage shoot production.

Gooseberries There are two prunings to be carried out on these thorny bushes. In summer shorten the sideshoots to about five leaves. In winter remove one or two older stems completely and shorten the remainder by half. Cut back sideshoots to three buds.

Peaches and nectarines One-year old maiden trees are trained as follows:

1. First winter: Plant the tree against a wall or fence equipped with horizontal wires 30-cm (1-ft) apart.

2. First spring: Cut back the stem to 60 cm (2 ft), making your cut just above a sprouting shoot. When two shoots start to grow in opposite directions low down on the bush, select these as your framework growths and cut back the main stem to just above them. Remove any other shoots that remain. Fasten a cane to the wires to mark the path of each shoot. They should run at an angle of 45 degrees from the main stem. Pinch out any sideshoots that form on your chosen laterals.

3. Second winter: Shorten the two laterals to 1 m (3 ft).

4. Second summer: Allow four evenly spaced shoots to grow from each of the laterals. Pinch out any sideshoots that appear on them.

5. Third winter: Cut the new laterals back to 1 m (3 ft).

6. Third summer: Allow sideshoots to grow from the established laterals at 23-cm (9-in) intervals, but only from the tops of the shoots. Pinch out any that grow on the undersides, or straight out from the wall. Pinch out the tips of the chosen shoots when they are 45 cm (18 in) long. The topmost bud that is left on each new lateral can then be allowed to grow on and extend the framework even further.

Fruit will be carried on one-year old wood, which can now be produced on the established framework. As soon as fruit is picked, cut out the fruited shoots and tie in new ones to replace them. Overcrowding shoots can be picked off while they are fresh and sappy in spring.

Plums, damsons and gages   All need little pruning once they are established. Young trees should have all their branches shortened by half their length in the early spring immediately after planting. Repeat the process the following spring, removing half of the previous season's growth. Apart from the removal of spindly shoots, this is all the formative pruning that should be necessary.

Always prune plums, damsons and gages in spring and summer. If pruned in winter they will be laid open to attack by silver leaf disease.

Raspberries   There are two distinct kinds of raspberry: the summer fruiters and the autumn fruiters. Summer fruiters carry their crop on canes made in the previous year. Autumn fruiters carry fruits on the current year's stems, so pruning is different.

Summer fruiters   Cut out all fruited canes down to soil level once the crop has been picked. Tie in the new canes to replace them.

Autumn fruiters   Cut all canes down to ground level in late winter.

Newly planted canes of both types are cut down to soil level in late winter. The summer fruiters will crop in their second year, the autumn fruiters in their first.

Pruning summer-fruiting raspberries

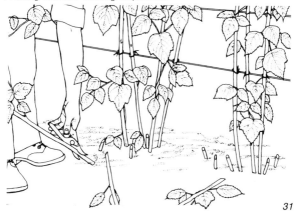

Index

*Page numbers in italics refer
to illustrations*

blackspot 3
bleeding 7, 10

colourful stems 6, 14, 22, *24*
cordons 5, 6, 7, 26
cutting 8

espalier 26
evergreens 6, 11, 16

fruit 26–31

hedges 8, 11, 12, 14, 17, 18,
    19, 21, 23

leader 7, 10
loppers 8

mildew 3

ornamental trees and shrubs
    10–25
overcrowded shoots 3, 22,
    29, 30

pruning saw 8

reverted stems 6

secateurs 2, 8
shears 8
shoot growth 6
silver leaf disease 31
spur system 5, *5*, 6
spurs 5, 6, 12, 26
suckers 14

timing 7
tools 8
topiary 19
tree pruning 7, 8, 14

variegated plants 6

wall-trained plants 11, 12,
    17, 20, 21, 29
wound sealant 8